W9-ARV-485

TAKING ACTION TO IMPROVE SCHOOLS

SABINA LAWSON

Lerner Publications ◆ Minneapolis

To Steven Miller.
You encouraged me,
inspired me, and
changed my life.

Lerner Publications Company
A division of Lerner Publishing Group, Inc.
241 First Avenue North
Minneapolis, MN USA 55401

For reading levels and more information, look up this title at www.lernerbooks.com.

Main body text set in Perpetua Std 13.5/18. Typeface provided by Monotype.

Library of Congress Cataloging-in-Publication Data

Names: Lawson, Sabina, author.
Title: Taking action to improve schools / Sabina Lawson.
Description: Minneapolis : Lerner Publications, [2016] | Series: Who's changing the world? |
    Audience: Age 9–12. | Audience: Grades 4–6. | Includes bibliographical references and index.
Identifiers: LCCN 2015036527| ISBN 9781467793933 (lb : alk. paper) | ISBN 9781467796668 (eb pdf)
Subjects: LCSH: Educators—Biography—Juvenile literature. | Teachers—Biography—
    Juvenile literature. | Educational change—Juvenile literature.
Classification: LCC LA2301 .W37 2016 | DDC 371.2/07—dc23
LC record available at http://lccn.loc.gov/2015036527

Manufactured in the United States of America
1 – VP – 7/15/16

CONTENTS

INTRODUCTION
IMPROVING SCHOOLS

A boy in Chicago spoke to his city. A girl in Michigan wore shorts. A boy in Canada collected school supplies. A girl in Pakistan wrote a blog. These kids all saw problems in their schools: there was not enough money, dress codes were discriminatory, some kids couldn't afford pencils and notebooks, and girls weren't allowed to learn. So they decided to take action to do something about these problems.

Education activists work to make sure all students have access to the same quality of education.

These aren't the only issues affecting education either. Some people think students have to take too many tests. Some students don't have enough money to attend school at all. Sometimes students don't have a good environment in which to learn. These issues can seem too big to fix—but lots of people are trying.

Activism comes in many different forms. People can organize protests, or they can write an article. Some people teach classes and

These activists in Chicago organized a protest to make a change.

start nonprofit organizations. Other people talk to their neighbors or give speeches.

You don't have to be a politician or a writer to be an activist. You don't have to be a teacher or a principal or a parent to see a problem in your school. You don't have to have lots of money or a college degree to take action. And you definitely don't have to be an adult to make a change. All you need is the desire to fix a problem and the willingness to try.

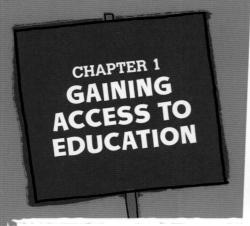

CHAPTER 1
GAINING ACCESS TO EDUCATION

Asean Johnson speaks to Chicago Public School leaders at a community meeting in 2013.

ASEAN JOHNSON
FUTURE MAYOR OF CHICAGO

In 2013 Asean Johnson was a normal third grader at Marcus Garvey Elementary School in Chicago, Illinois. Then the Chicago Public Schools system announced it was planning to cut teachers, and it threatened to close Asean's school.

At just nine years old, Asean felt he had a mission. In May he gave a speech at a Chicago rally protesting the school closings. Asean said that the school closings were racist because they would mostly affect African American students. He urged Chicago mayor Rahm Emanuel to support Chicago city schools, not close them. Asean's speech went viral. People watched the YouTube video of his speech more than 350,000 times.

His speech was so moving that Chicago Teachers Union president Karen Lewis said she would endorse him for mayor—when he turns twenty-one in 2025. "Just in case my basketball and football careers don't work, I'll have president, lawyer, and scientist as backup plans," Asean said. "Maybe mayor of Chicago."

Two months later, Asean gave another speech. He spoke to members of the Chicago Board of Education. He told the board that by closing his school, they were taking away his chance at a good education. As he spoke, tears streamed down his cheeks.

More than fifty Chicago schools were supposed to close. Only four stayed open. One of those schools was Asean's. After the school board voted to keep his school open, a reporter asked him, "Do you think you helped save your school?"

"Yes," Asean replied, "but I don't think it was just me. . . . It was the parents that came out and the students that came out to help Marcus Garvey."

Activists gathered at a rally to protest school closings in Chicago.

KATHLEEN MCGINN
NEGOTIATING AN EDUCATION

In Zambia, a country in Africa, many families live in poverty. Often families cannot afford to send their children to school. And female students face additional obstacles. If a family does send a daughter to school, they often also expect her to complete household tasks such as cooking and cleaning along with her schoolwork. A lot of girls are forced to drop out of school because of these many responsibilities.

When young girls drop out of school, they often do not have a way to support themselves. Instead, they are forced to rely on a man for financial support. These young girls are also less likely than men to receive health education. This leaves young girls vulnerable to becoming pregnant and getting diseases such as HIV. In 2015, 60 percent of people in Zambia were living in poverty and 14 percent of people had HIV.

Kathleen McGinn, a professor at Harvard Business School, wondered if the lack of education for students in Zambia was not only because of poverty. She wondered if it was a communication issue.

Together with two other professors, Corinne Low and Nava Ashraf, McGinn began researching what might happen if girls in Zambia were taught how to speak for themselves instead of having to rely on their families or older men to make decisions for them. They wrote lesson plans that would be used to teach girls how to negotiate. Girls in a region of Zambia called Lusaka can now take classes that teach them how to respectfully communicate what they want and brainstorm ways to achieve their goals.

Girls in class in Zambia

McGinn's research will take a few years, but for some girls, the negotiation skills have already been useful.

Madalitso Mulando has taken the negotiation class twice. When her

EVELYN ISHIOKWU

Evelyn Ishiokwu goes to school in Ajegunle, Nigeria. She says kids there don't like to go to school. Lots of kids drop out. Teenage girls often get pregnant, and there are gangs and lots of violence.

But Evelyn thinks it is important to finish school, and she wants her classmates to know this too. So she began helping her classmates with schoolwork and talking to them about education. She tells girls to be confident, and she tells boys not to be violent.

Evelyn's teachers are proud of her. They say that students' attitudes have changed, and their grades have improved because Evelyn was willing to speak up.

parents told her they couldn't afford $150 to send her to school, she put her skills to work. She called her cousin, her sister, and her uncle, and she explained that she wanted to finish her education. Between those relatives and her own parents, Madalitso came up with enough money to finish tenth grade and buy her textbooks.

McGinn, Low, and Ashraf hope that eventually negotiation classes will be taught all over Zambia and that this will change the cycle of poverty and lower the rates of unwanted pregnancy and HIV.

GEOFFREY CANADA
ENDING THE CYCLE OF POVERTY

Geoffrey Canada knows what it's like to have nothing. He grew up in the South Bronx, New York. His father left the family when Geoffrey was very young, so the boy's mother raised him and his three brothers on her own. They lived in a building filled with cockroaches and rats.

Geoffrey Canada helps kids in Harlem, New York, get out of poverty.

Often the family had no heat or hot water.

When Canada was a teenager, he made a promise to himself. If he made it out of poverty, he'd come back to help other kids do the same. Canada kept his promise. He graduated from Bowdoin College and the Harvard Graduate School of Education. In 1990 he became president and CEO of Harlem Children's Zone.

Harlem is one of the poorest places in New York. Many students there can't see a way out of poverty and don't know that they could have a future outside of Harlem. Often they don't get a good education because their schools don't have enough resources or can't afford dedicated teachers. With Harlem Children's Zone, Canada is trying to break the cycle of poverty and give kids a better life.

Harlem Children's Zone starts to help children even before they're born. It offers women pregnancy classes so their babies are born healthy. Children can start in the program's preschool classes at the age of three, and they can attend charter schools from kindergarten through twelfth grade. Classes are small, and kids get a free breakfast, lunch, and snack at school. Because of funding and resources, these programs are small. Many of them have waiting lists, and admission to the charter schools is by lottery. Students who aren't chosen for the charter schools can take part in after-school programs for tutoring and to get help planning for college.

In 2014 the program helped more than thirteen thousand kids get a better education. More than eight hundred Harlem Children's Zone students were in college, and one hundred more had just graduated. Canada served as the head of Harlem Children's Zone until 2014, but he is still very involved in its programs. His work and leadership live on in the program that continues to help kids learn and break free from poverty.

A dorm building on the campus of Princeton University

CATHARINE BELLINGER AND ALEXIS MORIN

OVERCOMING INEQUALITY

When Catharine Bellinger began attending Princeton University in 2008, she looked for a group to join that was interested in discussing education. She couldn't find one. So she e-mailed other students in the teacher education program to see if any shared her special interest in education policies. Fellow freshman Alexis Morin answered her e-mail.

While Bellinger was in high school in Washington, DC, she volunteered at schools and even taught a high school math class. Morin had been a representative on the school board in her hometown of Northborough, Massachusetts. Both Morin and Bellinger had seen firsthand that there were problems in education. Lots of students in the United States weren't able to go to good schools or learn from excellent teachers. Students who came from poor families or who were not white often struggled more in school than did white students from wealthy families.

So they decided to start a club at Princeton called Students for Education Reform (SFER). Their group would educate other college students about problems in education. It would also encourage these college students to write articles, vote, and talk to decision makers about schools.

In 2011 SFER became an official nonprofit organization. By the end of the year, it had spread to twenty other schools and had one thousand participants. By 2012 there were more than one hundred groups in thirty-three states. Morin and Bellinger decided they would both take a year off from school to begin running the organization full-time.

One of the group's main goals is to turn college students into future leaders. Morin and Bellinger believe that more top students need to become teachers and school leaders. In these roles, they can improve schools in their cities and towns. They can change school policies so that better teachers are hired and students receive a better education. They can make sure teachers are paid well. And they can work to overcome inequality in schools.

Since 2009 SFER has worked on thirteen issues in twenty-two states. They have helped to write policies about teacher evaluations in Minnesota and Connecticut, and their members have become involved with school board elections in California and Colorado.

Morin stayed with Students for Education Reform, and she now serves as its executive director. In 2014 Bellinger moved on to another organization called Democrats for Education Reform (DFER). Like SFER, this group works to change the American education system so that all children have access to excellent education.

PEGGY ROBERTSON
TOO MANY TESTS

Each year students in the United States take standardized tests. These tests are meant to show how well students are learning in subjects like math, science, and reading. These are sometimes called high-stakes tests. That's because, in some places, if students get low scores on the tests, the government might decide the school isn't doing a good job of teaching students. The school might lose funding. Some teachers may lose their jobs.

Students in the United States take many standardized tests each year.

Peggy Robertson taught elementary school for many years. She thought students were taking too many tests. She also didn't think the tests were working. She believed that many students stopped enjoying school because they were tested so often.

Many other teachers and parents agreed with Robertson. They said that standardized tests were causing students too much stress. They said that teachers spent too much time teaching subjects that would be on the test, such as math and history. Students had less time to spend on other subjects like art and physical education. Parents, students, and teachers around the country began protesting standardized tests. So the opt-out movement began.

In 2011 Robertson and a few other people joined together to help people learn how they could opt out of, or not take, standardized tests.

First, Robertson's team started a Facebook page called United Opt Out. They posted files about testing in all fifty states. These files described the tests and laws in each state. They also gave people examples of letters to write to schools about why they chose not to take the tests.

Robertson also wrote a blog about education and testing called *Peg with Pen*. On her blog, she began encouraging her readers to participate in the

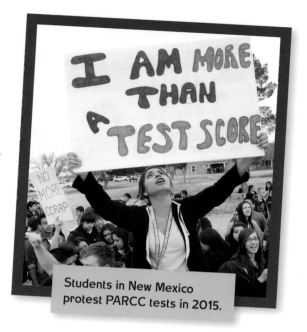

Students in New Mexico protest PARCC tests in 2015.

opt-out movement. In August 2011, she wrote about the first organized United Opt Out action—people all around the country would write articles about why they chose to opt out. They would publish these articles in their local newspapers.

Three years later, Robertson was still writing about standardized tests. She published an article saying that she refused to give her students in Colorado a standardized test called Partnership for Assessment of Readiness for College and Careers (PARCC). She said preparing for this test made her less able to help her students. They would only learn how to memorize information, not how to think or solve problems on their own. She believes that these tests are making the gap between success rates of students from different racial and economic backgrounds worse, not better. Writing this article put Robertson's job at risk, but she said, "We must be the change. Sometimes change requires risk."

United Opt Out continued to offer support to teachers, parents, and students who were against standardized tests. More teachers are refusing to give the tests. Parents are allowing their children to skip them. Students are boycotting them. At one school in Seattle, Washington, the entire eleventh-grade class did not come to school on a testing day in April 2015.

School officials have fought back, saying these tests are important. But the opt-out movement will not give up and shows no signs of slowing down.

SARAH MYERS-LEVITT
DISTRACTING DRESS CODES

"For the past three years of my life, dress code has distracted me more than anything else at school," said Sarah Myers-Levitt, an eighth grader at Forsythe Middle School in Ann Arbor, Michigan. "Constantly making sure my shirt is pulled down in the hall and avoiding certain teachers, getting called down to the office to change . . ."

Some US middle schools place guidelines on the length of shorts and skirts their students wear.

Dress code has become one of the most frustrating parts of school for some students in the United States. Many schools have rules for how long shirts and skirts need to be. They ban leggings and yoga pants. Shoulders can't be bare. Hats must not be worn. Often schools say that these rules help students learn better— free from the distractions of clothing choices. But some students say that these rules are more distracting than the clothes themselves.

Sarah said that the dress code at her school isn't fair. Sometimes her school gets hot. She would like to be able to wear shorts so she can be comfortable. Sometimes she feels that girls get called out more often than boys for wearing inappropriate clothing. Boys might get a warning when their T-shirts are inappropriate, but girls may be kept out of class until they change. In May 2015, Sarah decided she was tired of these inconsistencies.

First, she posted about the dress code on Instagram. Then she organized a protest with eighty other students. They all came to school wearing clothes that were against the dress code. Girls wore shorts, and boys wore muscle shirts.

Later, in a letter to parents, the principal of Forsythe Middle School described the incident. Students who participated in the protest were asked to change. Some of their parents were called, but nobody was punished. Instead, teachers met with all the students and allowed them to voice their concerns about the dress code. The principal invited parents to give feedback and promised that the school would consider parent and student ideas and update the dress code.

According to Sarah, a few days later, some girls wore the same shorts they had worn in the protest. The teachers didn't say anything.

At the beginning of the next school year, the dress code posted on Forsythe Middle School's website stated that students are to dress in a manner that is respectful and appropriate. Shoulder straps are to be 2 inches (5 centimeters) wide, and shorts must be mid-thigh length. Leggings and yoga pants are allowed as long as they are worn with a long shirt, skirt, or dress, and students who violate the dress code will be treated with respect and given the option to change or call a parent to bring a change of clothes.

LEONIE HAIMSON
STOP OVERCROWDING SCHOOLS

In 1996 Leonie Haimson's son started first grade in New York City. He was put in a class with twenty-eight other children. Haimson thought the class was way too big. She believes that smaller classes improve children's ability to learn. Class size also reduces bad behavior and helps kids graduate on time. Many studies of class size show that students learn better in classes with fewer than twenty students. In small classes, students are more likely to stay interested in what they are learning.

Large classes, on the other hand, can be difficult for teachers to handle. They sometimes feel overwhelmed, and students can feel unimportant. Some schools do not have enough space for all the students, so kids have to stand or have class in hallways and closets.

Haimson wanted to make sure that her son and other New York City

(*From left*) Michael Meyers, Director of the New York Civil Rights Coalition, Norman Siegel, civil rights attorney, and Leonie Haimson at an education rally in New York.

kids did not suffer from overcrowded schools. So she started the parent group Class Size Matters. It encourages schools around the country to make classes smaller. The group also works to make sure the public is educated about the benefits of small classes. Haimson, who blogs and writes articles for *Huffington Post* and edits the *NYC Public School Parents* blog, has also become involved in other education issues. She writes about school funding, the achievement gap, and standardized testing. In addition, she started two other organizations, Parent Coalition for Student Privacy and Parents Across America (PAA). The Parent Coalition seeks to make sure that student information and data is not shared without their permission. PAA strives to give parents a voice in their children's education.

Class Size Matters has made progress, but it still has a long way to go. In 2014 reports showed that in New York, the average class size for kindergarten through third grade dropped slightly, from 24.9 in 2013 to 24.7 in 2014, and the size of fourth- through eighth-grade classes also dropped from 26.8 to 26.7—yet high school classes grew. And despite the drops in the younger grades, 30,444 kindergarten students (43 percent) were still in classes of 25 or more. More than 350,000 students of all ages were still in classes of 30 or more. This was up from the previous year.

In March 2015, Haimson testified before the New York City Council Committee on Education, saying that schools are still overcrowded. She is not giving up in her fight for smaller class sizes and better education for students. She told the education committee, "Only with significantly improved planning, policies, and funding can our public school students be provided with the learning opportunities they deserve."

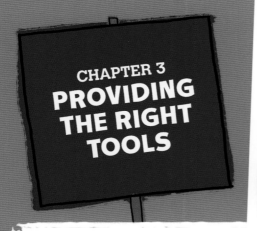

CHAPTER 3
PROVIDING THE RIGHT TOOLS

Stephen McPhee in 2015

STEPHEN MCPHEE
BACKPACKS FOR THE HOMELESS

More than 1.6 million American children in 2015 found themselves without a place to call home. Homeless families often move from shelter to shelter. Each time they change shelters, their children must go to a new school and start over. They must get used to new teachers and make new friends. Homeless kids also struggle to afford basic school supplies like clothes, pencils, and notebooks. These kids often struggle in school and score lower on tests than students who live in permanent homes.

In December 2006, Stephen McPhee overheard his parents talking about the homeless children in and around Calgary, in Alberta, Canada, where they lived. Stephen wanted to help these children. Together Stephen and his parents packed fifteen backpacks full of school supplies, personal hygiene items, toys, and other things homeless kids needed. They delivered the backpacks to Inn from the Cold, a homeless shelter in Calgary. Stephen wanted to do more, but he was only six years old. He decided to tell everyone about his dream to help the homeless, to try to get more adults to help.

A story about Stephen's mission appeared in a local newspaper. People who read his story were moved by it. They donated 265 backpacks to shelters in Calgary. In 2008 a charity called Stephen's Backpacks for Children in Need Society formed. That year the society helped give six hundred pairs of shoes to poor children, and the premier (leader) of Alberta presented Stephen with an Alberta's Great Kids Award. In 2011 Stephen delivered 2,500 backpacks to homeless kids, and the next year, he received Alberta's Generosity of Spirit Award.

In 2010 Stephen helped deliver twenty-five hundred backpacks to homeless kids.

By the time Stephen was an eighth grader, his charity had helped more than thirty-one thousand homeless kids. Stephen is still committed to his dream. A news reporter once asked Stephen how long he will keep helping homeless children. He said he will help until there are no more homeless kids.

HANNAH GODEFA
WRITING TO ETHIOPIA

Hannah Godefa was born in Canada. But her family had come to Canada from Ethiopia, one of the poorest countries in the world. When she was seven years old, Hannah went with her parents to visit their hometown of Axum, a city in northern Ethiopia. Hannah made friends with the kids there and wanted to write them letters once she returned home. But the Ethiopian children could not afford pencils and paper to write back to her.

Hannah Godefa at a UNICEF event in 2014

Hannah believed that something as small as a lack of pencils should not stop children from learning. So she started a project called Pencil Mountain. It started as a donation drive at her elementary school. Then her program grew. They delivered almost half a million pencils and other school supplies to children in rural Ethiopia. The program also sent wheelchairs to help children with disabilities go to school. Later, Pencil Mountain sent science and technology books for high school and university students.

In 2013 a youth association in Ethiopia asked Hannah if she could help them build a youth center. Hannah set up a fund to help raise money for the youth center and other organizations in Ethiopia. That year Hannah became a UNICEF national ambassador to

Hannah delivers a speech at the Girl Summit 2014 in England.

Ethiopia. UNICEF is a charity that helps poor children around the world. Hannah visited children in Ethiopia to find out how UNICEF can better help them with health, nutrition, and education. She also discovered other ways to use her voice to speak up for children's right to education. At the age of seventeen, Hannah works with UNICEF to raise awareness about education for girls in poor countries. According to her website, "Hannah does not want a world where all children are happy and safe to be just a dream, but a reality."

CHRISTIAN BOER
A NEW WAY TO READ

Dyslexia is a condition that makes it difficult for some people's brains to recognize symbols properly. Sometimes letters seem to flip around, or they just look the same as other letters. People who have dyslexia often have a hard time reading. They need to read slowly or guess at words because their brains don't recognize words quickly. More than 10 percent of people in the world have dyslexia.

Christian Boer, an artist from the Netherlands, has dyslexia. He knows how frustrating it can be for students in school to have dyslexia. They might read more slowly than their classmates, and they sometimes fall behind. For a long time, Boer tried to ignore his dyslexia, but he also knows that it's important for kids to read a lot. So he started thinking about solutions instead.

While he was a student at the Utrecht Art Academy in 2008, one of his teachers encouraged his ideas for trying to make it easier for people with dyslexia to read. Boer worked for six months to develop a new font, or way of writing letters in books and on computers. The font is called Dyslexie, and in this font, each letter is completely unique, so it's harder to confuse them. The letters are slanted in different ways, there is more space between them, and they look thicker in some places so that the brain doesn't flip them around.

Christian Boer developed a font to help people with dyslexia read more easily.

Information and excitement about the Dyslexie font spread quickly. Two universities researched and tested Dyslexie. They found out that three-quarters of people with dyslexia were able to read faster and with fewer mistakes when they used the Dyslexie font. People started to talk about the font in the news and online. Businesses and schools began contacting Boer to buy the font. In 2012 the first book was published in Dyslexie. By 2014 the font was becoming popular all around the world. By 2015 more than one thousand books had been published using Dyslexie.

Boer hopes that his font will help raise awareness about dyslexia. To further his goal, he made sure that Dyslexie can be downloaded from his website and used for free at schools and in people's homes.

CHAPTER 4
FIGHTING FOR CULTURAL AWARENESS

A crowd of students greets Jonathan Butler (*center*) at the end of his seven-day hunger strike.

JONATHAN BUTLER
HUNGRY FOR CHANGE

Jonathan Butler said that from the moment he stepped onto the campus of Missouri State University (MSU) in Columbia, Missouri, as a freshman in 2008, he did not feel safe. Butler is African American, and from the time he first enrolled, he says he heard racist comments from other students. Both afraid and concerned, Butler began to get involved in activism. When an African American man was killed by a police officer in a town two hours away, Butler and some friends drove there to protest.

In 2015 Butler was still at MSU. He had decided that he wanted to become even more involved in his community by getting a degree in education and becoming a school leader and advocate for education. That year racism at MSU became even more obvious to Butler.

On several occasions, students yelled racist things to African Americans on campus. Butler became frustrated because he said it took school leaders a long time to respond to these incidents. "It's just a very hostile environment for black students," he noted. "We are facing a lot of negativity and oppression on a daily basis . . . our lives are still not valued."

On October 10, Butler and some other students decided to protest at the MSU homecoming parade. They hoped that MSU's president, Tim Wolfe, would listen and respond to the racism on campus. Instead, the students felt that Wolfe ignored them.

Butler decided that he needed to do something big. On Monday, November 2, he announced that he would not eat until Wolfe was no longer the president of MSU.

Other students supported Butler. They set up their own protests and walkouts. The football team even announced that they would not play another game until Butler ended his strike. Butler's body became weak. He said he was prepared to die.

"I don't think Tim Wolfe is worth my life," he said. "But I do believe that when it comes to fighting justice, you have to be willing to have a level of sacrifice."

Monday, November 9, Wolfe resigned and Butler ended his strike. It had been an entire week since Butler had eaten any food. He was triumphant, but he said it wasn't about him. He asked his fellow students not to focus on the hunger strike but on the problem of racism.

"It should not have taken this much," he said. "And it is disgusting and vile that we find ourselves in a place that we do."

SHELBY SNYDER
POCAHONTAS PETITION

One week before the Disney-themed homecoming parade at Copper Hills High School in West Jordan, Utah, Shelby Snyder found out that one of the floats would be a Pocahontas float. Shelby is a junior at Copper Hills. She is also the president of the school's American Indian Student Association.

Shelby thought the float, which featured a tipi and girls dressed in fringed dresses, was insensitive toward American Indians. She complained to the school, but she was told that there was not enough time to change the float.

The day after the parade, Shelby went to the homecoming football game and collected 190 signatures on a petition asking for cultural awareness and tolerance. "Our culture is not your costume," Shelby said. "When people dress up as Pocahontas, it just makes it seem like they're mocking our culture and making fun of [it]."

A few days later, the principal of Copper Hills High School, Todd Quarnberg, apologized. "Copper Hills High embraces diversity, and we want an inclusive environment for every student," he said. The school also announced that it is working to educate both staff and students about cultural sensitivity.

CURTIS ACOSTA
EMPOWERING MINORITY STUDENTS

For many years, Curtis Acosta taught Mexican American studies courses in schools in Tucson, Arizona. His students discussed poetry, books, and music written by people of color. They thought about history and culture from a perspective that is often overlooked in schools—the perspective of minorities. Studies showed that the Mexican American studies courses helped students achieve better grades. Fewer students dropped out of school, and more went to college.

But in 2010, the Arizona government banned the course. They thought the class was teaching students to act against the American government. Acosta was not allowed to teach the things he had taught for years. He even had his books taken away. "They took away everything; we were banned from our own curriculum, our intellect, our own selves," Acosta said. "It was dehumanizing."

Curtis Acosta lectures during his Latino literature class in Arizona.

For a while, Acosta continued teaching a similar class outside of school on Sundays. He even partnered with a local college so that his students could receive college credit for the class. Acosta also met with school leaders, wrote articles and letters, and joined with ten other teachers to challenge the law in court. But eventually, Acosta resigned from teaching in Tucson. "I gave it a shot, and it was painful," he said.

But the issue was far from over. In 2013 the federal court ordered Tucson schools to reinstate culturally relevant classes. That wasn't the only victory. A teacher in Los Angeles heard about the situation and decided to start ethnic studies courses in California. A professor in Texas did the same. And Acosta went on to start his own education consulting business, called Acosta Latino Learning Partnership. He helps start ethnic studies programs in schools across the country.

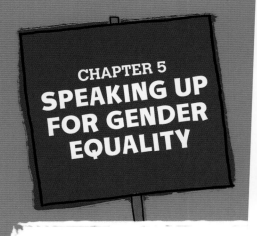

CHAPTER 5
SPEAKING UP FOR GENDER EQUALITY

Malala Yousafzai after accepting the Nobel Peace Prize in 2014

MALALA YOUSAFZAI
A GIRL'S RIGHT TO EDUCATION

Malala Yousafzai was born in the Swat Valley area of Pakistan in 1997. At first, she had a pretty normal life with her family. She went to the school her father had started. Then the Taliban began to take control of the area where she lived. The Taliban is a radical Islamic group run by men. Women and girls have almost no rights under the Taliban. They are not allowed to go to school or to work.

Malala did not want to stop going to school. When the Taliban began to attack girls' schools in the area where she lived, Malala stood up to them. She spoke out in the media about her belief that all girls have the right to an education. She wrote a blog about her experience. To hide from the Taliban, she wrote under the name Gul Makai, which comes from an old Pakistani folk story. People around the world heard Malala's message. In 2011 she received the first ever National Youth Peace Prize in Pakistan.

The Taliban did not like what Malala had to say. They issued a death threat against her. On October 9, 2012, Malala was on a bus riding home from school. A Taliban man stopped the bus and boarded. He asked for her by name. When the man identified Malala, he shot her. The bullet went through the side of her head and into her shoulder. Two other girls on the bus were also hurt.

The bullet damaged Malala's skull and left her in a coma. She was taken to Birmingham, England, for medical care. Once she had recovered, Malala began attending school in England. Even after the attack, Malala stood up against the Taliban. She would not stop speaking out about girls' right to an education.

People in Pakistan and around the world were moved by Malala's bravery. More than two million people in Pakistan signed a petition for the Right to Education campaign. That campaign led to a bill that guaranteed a free education to all Pakistanis—boys and girls.

Malala became a symbol of girls' rights around the world. In 2013 she started the Malala Fund to raise money and awareness and to help young girls around the world go to school. In 2014 she became the youngest person ever to win a Nobel Peace Prize. In 2015 the well-known American director Davis Guggenheim made a documentary about her story called *He Named Me Malala*. Malala continues to be an inspiration for women and girls all around the world.

COY MATHIS
ACHIEVING FAIR TREATMENT

Coy Mathis was born a boy. But Coy didn't like playing with tanks or cars as some boys do. Instead, he loved his pink stuffed pony.

In fact, he loved just about anything pink—including the pink tutu he often wore. Coy's parents discovered their son is transgender. Though he was born with a boy's body, inside he feels like a girl. So Coy's parents let him dress in girls' clothes, paint his bedroom pink, and live as a girl.

This made Coy very happy. Then, in December 2012, when Coy was in first grade, her parents got a call from the principal of her Colorado elementary school. The principal said Coy would no longer be allowed to use the girls' bathroom. Some of the parents had complained. Coy did not feel comfortable using the boys' bathroom because she identifies as a girl.

The Mathis family pulled Coy out of the school. They filed a discrimination complaint with the Colorado Civil Rights Division. Coy's parents said that the school was not treating Coy fairly or with respect by making her use a bathroom she didn't feel comfortable using. The Mathis family won. Coy would be allowed to use the girls' bathroom. It was the first time a transgender student earned the right to use the bathroom of the gender they feel inside. Even after the Mathis family won, they decided to move Coy to a more tolerant place. In second grade, Coy switched to a new school

Coy was honored at the annual GLAAD Media Awards in 2013.

near Denver, Colorado, that fully accepted her as a girl.

In time, Coy's story spread. She went on TV and appeared at a fundraiser for a gay, lesbian, bisexual, and transgender advocacy group called GLAAD (formerly the Gay & Lesbian Alliance Against Defamation). Coy became a voice for other transgender children fighting for their right to be treated fairly.

GENDER AND SCHOOL BATHROOMS

Going to the bathroom at school might not seem like a big deal, but it can be an uncomfortable situation for transgender kids. Kids like Coy Mathis are often forced to use the bathroom of the gender they were born—not the gender they feel like inside. This can be embarrassing for them.

In August 2013, California governor Jerry Brown signed a bill into law known as the School Bathroom Bill. It was the first law in the country to allow transgender students to use the bathrooms and locker rooms they feel most comfortable using.

MADDY PAIGE BAXTER
TACKLING SCHOOL SPORTS

Like many kids, Madison (Maddy) Paige Baxter loves sports, especially football. She plays defensive tackle. Her job is to block the player with the ball to prevent a touchdown.

Maddy has been playing football since she was seven years old. Her dream is to get a scholarship and become one of the first female college football players. The twelve-year-old was a standout on her middle school football team in Locust Grove, Georgia. But just as she was about to start seventh grade, Maddy's school asked her to leave the team.

The head of her school, Patrick Stuart, said Maddy could not play because boys and girls should not be on the same sports teams. He was afraid Maddy might hear some bad language in the locker room. He also feared the boys might treat Maddy differently from other players.

Maddy and her mother started a Facebook campaign called Let Her Play to support Maddy's mission to play football. The page went viral. In just one week, it got more than thirty thousand "likes" and lots of positive comments. Members of the US Women's National football team left messages of support. Maddy vowed to keep playing football, even if her school wouldn't let her back on the team. She said she'd play on a local recreational team if she had to. Or she would switch schools.

KICKED OUT FOR PLAYING SPORTS WITH A GIRL

A few decades ago, the idea of a girl playing on a boys' sports team might have raised eyebrows. These days, it's become more common for girls to play on boys' teams. But not everyone is happy about the idea of coed teams.

In August 2015, a Virginia youth basketball team called the Charlottesville Cavaliers made it into the semifinals of the National Travel Basketball Association's (NTBA's) championship tournament. But before the team could shoot a single basket, they were disqualified. Why? The Cavaliers had a girl on the team—Kymora Johnson. The NTBA has a rule that no girls can play on teams with boys in national tournament games.

Ten-year-old Kymora volunteered to sit out the game. But the officials were firm in their decision. The Cavaliers would be disqualified, and a team they had already beaten would play in the semifinals instead. Kymora's team held a silent protest. They showed up to the game they would have played and stood on the sidelines wearing pink jerseys to support Kymora.

Maddy's school would not budge on their decision, and in the end, Maddy decided to be homeschooled instead. She joined a coed recreational team that she says is actually a tougher league than the one her school was in. Maddy will continue to fight for gender equality. "All athletes should play to their ability and not their gender," she said.

CHARLOTTE MURPHY
FIGHTING FOR TITLE IX

In 2012 eleven-year-old Charlotte Murphy was a fourth grader at Linden Elementary School in Pittsburgh, Pennsylvania. One day, she learned that her school was planning to cut her basketball team. But the boys' team would not be cut. Charlotte did not think that was fair.

She wrote a letter to Linda Lane, the superintendent of Pittsburgh Public Schools. She told Lane that canceling the girls' team violated Title IX. This civil rights law prevents schools and other public groups from discriminating based on gender. Charlotte asked to have a meeting with the superintendent.

Charlotte's letter impressed the school superintendent. Lane invited Charlotte to her office for a meeting. After the meeting, Lane changed the rules at Pittsburgh Public Schools. From then on, if a school wanted to have a boys' sports team, it also had to have a girls' team for the same sport. The district went from having three girls' basketball teams to having fourteen teams. At one school, forty girls showed up for tryouts!

CHAPTER 6

MAKING SCHOOLS SAFE

Jake Ross at a Minnesota Senate Education Committee hearing in 2013

JAKE ROSS
A NEW LAW

School was no fun for second grader Jake Ross. Two of his classmates at Forest Lake Elementary School in Minnesota did awful things to him every day. They hit him in the hallways and stole his backpack. At recess one day, they beat Jake up and pushed him to the ground over and over again. One of the boys warned Jake that he'd kill him if he told his teachers about the attack.

Jake was afraid to go to school. His mom also worried about his safety. She reported the incidents to the school. She asked if the school had any rules about bullying. It did not have any rules. The bullying did not stop.

Instead of giving in, Jake fought back. He became an anti-bullying activist. Jake took his story straight to the Minnesota State Capitol. He told a group of senators about the bullying he had endured. He urged them to pass a new law to keep Minnesota schoolchildren safe.

Jake Ross watches Governor Mark Dayton sign the Safe and Supportive Minnesota Schools Act into law in 2014.

On April 9, 2014, Minnesota governor Mark Dayton signed the Safe and Supportive Minnesota Schools Act into law. The law requires schools to protect students from bullying. Schools must teach kids who bully why their behavior is wrong and show them how to act appropriately toward their classmates. This law was a big accomplishment for Jake. He gave a speech at the signing event, and the crowd cheered.

NICOLE HOCKLEY AND MARK BARDEN
BUILDING A STRONGER COMMUNITY

December 14, 2012, started out as just another day at Sandy Hook Elementary School in Newtown, Connecticut. At 9:30 a.m., the students sat in their classrooms. They listened to the morning's announcements over the loudspeaker. Suddenly, they heard gunshots over the speaker.

A mentally ill young man named Adam Lanza had broken into the school and started shooting. Lanza killed twenty-six people in the school that day. Twenty of those who died were first-grade students.

Nicole Hockley's son was one of those first-grade students. Hockley and her family lived across the street from Lanza and his mother. Hockley didn't know the Lanzas very well, but she wondered how things might have been different if Adam Lanza had been more involved in the community.

Mark Barden's son was also killed on December 14. He too recognized that things could have been different for Lanza. "[Lanza]

Nicole Hockley speaks at an event for the Brady Center to Prevent Gun Violence in 2014.

was the kid that sat alone at the lunch table," he said. "I can't help but wonder [what might've been] if someone, anyone, had gone over to him and asked, 'Would you like to join us?'"

Hockley and Barden both decided to take action to be more inclusive and build a stronger community. "I do not want there to be a next time," Hockley said.

Days after the shooting, parents of Sandy Hook students and members of the Newtown community joined together to form an organization called Sandy Hook Promise (SHP). Barden and Hockley are both directors of the organization. The mission of SHP is to build strong communities, protect children, and reduce gun violence so that no more innocent lives are lost.

One of SHP's programs is called Start with Hello. This program teaches students how to be friendly and to include everyone in their conversations and play. By encouraging students to say hello and get to know their peers, Barden and Hockley hope that they are building a community in which people listen to one another and students like Lanza do not get overlooked.

Another program called Say Something teaches students to recognize signs of people who may be thinking about harming themselves or others. If students are able to recognize these signs and know who to talk to about them, perhaps school violence can be reduced.

SHP also works to educate the public about gun violence. As of 2014, SHP had educated almost two hundred community organizations about gun violence and SHP's programs. They had eight hundred

Hockley speaks at the Sandy Hook Promise launch in 2013.

volunteer leaders in twenty-three states raising awareness and leading SHP programs. SHP has more than 450,000 supporters, and they have reached 146,000 students through the Say Something and Start with Hello programs.

Barden and Hockley hope that more than anything else, SHP will encourage people to begin having respectful conversations and truly listen to one another.

ARCHER HADLEY
RAISING AWARENESS WITH WHEELCHAIRS

Archer Hadley was born with cerebral palsy, a condition that affects muscle strength and movement. Because Archer's brain can't control his muscles very well, it's hard for him to walk. He uses a wheelchair to get around his Austin, Texas, high school.

On one rainy day, Archer pulled up to one of the school's outside doors. He sat there for many minutes, trying to open the door with his free hand as rain rushed down his back. As he got wetter and more frustrated, Archer wondered why his school didn't have automatic doors for people with disabilities.

He asked his school to install three automatic doors. The trouble was that the doors cost more than $5,000 each. So Archer came up with an idea to raise money. His idea was called the Mr. Maroo Challenge. In this challenge, students at Archer's high school would challenge one another to spend an entire day in a wheelchair. They would pay $20 to put someone else in a wheelchair. The challenge was fun for students and also taught them about some of the challenges students with disabilities face. Archer said that after the challenge, his fellow students understood why automatic doors were necessary.

Archer's goal was to raise $40,000. Instead, he raised $87,000. The school was able to install five automatic doors. Archer also helped two other Austin high schools raise money to buy automatic doors.

Archer's success moved a lot of people—including Texas governor Greg Abbott. "Anyone with heart, anyone with determination, anyone with focus on achieving anything can achieve things beyond their wildest dreams. Archer is an inspiration, an inspiration for me, an inspiration for so many others," the governor said.

WHAT CAN *YOU* DO?

Each of the activists in this book has made a real difference in students' lives. They have fought to make schools safer. They have pushed to give equality to kids of different ethnicities and genders. They have worked to help poor students attain the same quality of education as wealthy students.

Sometimes it might seem scary to become an activist. Maybe you feel as if you're too young. Maybe you are afraid that no one will listen to you. Maybe you aren't sure you want to have a protest, or giving a speech makes you nervous.

That's okay. Anyone can become an education activist. And there are lots of different ways to make a difference. If you notice a problem in your school that you think needs solving, it's worth it to speak up for what you believe is right.

Maybe you notice that someone in your class is being left out or that other kids are making fun of someone. Maybe you see racial inequality in your school. Maybe it frustrates you to know that girls in countries across the world don't have access to an education.

You can start by simply talking to your friends, a parent, or your teachers about the problem. You can post something on social media, as Sarah Myers-Levitt did. You can write a letter, as Charlotte Murphy did. You can use your voice, as Asean Johnson did.

Or you can take action in other ways. Run for student council in your school. Tutor kids who need a little extra help in school. Start a fun challenge to raise awareness, as Archer Hadley did. Donate school supplies to those who are poor, as Stephen McPhee and Hannah Godefa did.

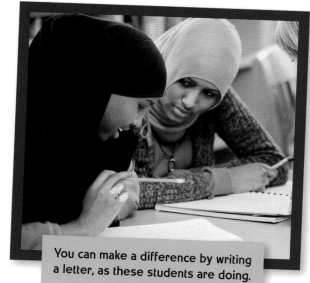

You can make a difference by writing a letter, as these students are doing.

The problems and the possibilities are endless. Give it a shot—you just might change the world.

Source Notes

7   Mark Konkol, "Asean Johnson Helped Save His School, Next Stop: Mayor?" DNAinfo, May 23, 2013, http://www.dnainfo.com/chicago/20130523 /washington-heights/asean-johnson-9-on-saving-his-school-fight-for-what-you-love.

7   Ibid.

15 Valerie Strauss, "Colorado Teacher: 'I Refuse to Administer the PARCC' Common Core Test to My Students," *Washington Post*, September 23, 2014, https://www .washingtonpost.com/news/answer-sheet/wp/2014/09/23/colorado-teacher-i -refuse-to-administer-the-parcc-common-core-test-to-my-students.

16 Lindsay Knake, "Students Protest Ann Arbor Middle School Dress Code," *MLive*, June 8, 2015, http://www.mlive.com/news/ann-arbor/index.ssf/2015/06 /students_protest_ann_arbor_mid.html.

19 Leonie Haimson, "Testimony of Leonie Haimson before the NYC Council Education Committee on School Overcrowding and the Deficiencies of the Capital Plan," Class Size Matters, March 3, 2015, http://www.classsizematters.org /testimony-of-leonie-haimson-before-the-nyc-council-education-committee-on -school-overcrowding-and-the-deficiencies-of-the-capital-plan.

23 "Education Is the Key to Success," Hannah Godefa Project, accessed October 26, 2015, http://www.hannahgodefa.com/hannahstory.

27 Michael E. Miller, "Black Grad Student on Hunger Strike in Mo. after Swastika Drawn with Human Feces," *Washington Post,* November 6, 2015, https://www .washingtonpost.com/news/morning-mix/wp/2015/11/06/black-grad -student-on-hunger-strike-in-mo-after-swastika-drawn-with-human-feces.

27 Ibid.

27 Jon Schuppe, "Jonathan Butler: How a Grad Student's Hunger Strike Toppled a University President," *NBC News*, November 10, 2015, http://www.nbcnews .com/news/us-news/jonathan-butler-how-grad-students-hunger-strike -toppled-university-president-n460161.

28 Benjamin Wood, "Utah School's 'Pocahontas' Parade Float Has Some Calling for Cultural Education," *Salt Lake Tribune*, September 29, 2015, http://www.sltrib .com/news/3001960-155/pocahontas-float-costumes-in-utah-school?fullpage=1.

28 Ibid.

29 Jing Fong, "When This Teacher's Ethnic Studies Classes Were Banned, His Students Took the District to Court—and Won," *yes! Magazine,* April 25, 2014, http:// www.yesmagazine.org/issues/education-uprising/interview-with-curtis-acosta.

29 Ibid.

35   Rebecca Klein, "Maddy Paige, 12, Kicked Off Male Football Team, Switches to Home Schooling," *Huffington Post*, July 24, 2013, http://www.huffingtonpost .com/2013/07/24/maddy-paige-homeschool_n_3645015.html.

38   Mark Barden, "After Newtown Tragedy, Honoring My Son with Conversation," *Huffington Post*, last modified February 11, 2014, http://www.huffingtonpost .com/mark-barden/after-newtown-tragedy-honoring-my-son-with -conversation_b_4428401.html.

38   John Christoffersen, "Sandy Hook Promise: Group Launches Anti-Violence Initiative," *Huffington Post*, January 14, 2013, http://www.huffingtonpost .com/2013/01/14/sandy-hook-promise_n_2474155.html.

41   "How a Wheelchair Challenge Mobilized a High School to Become More Accessible," *PBS NewsHour*, March 20, 2015, http://www.pbs.org/newshour /bb/wheelchair-challenge-mobilized-high-school-become-accessible.

Glossary

activist: a person who works to create change

charter school: a school that is run by teachers or parents. These schools receive public funding but do not have to follow as many rules of a city or state as other public schools do.

discriminate: to treat someone differently or deny them rights because of factors such as their gender, age, or race

documentary: a film that tells the facts about something

hygiene: practices that keep a person clean, such as brushing teeth or taking a shower

nonprofit: a business that uses the extra money it earns to achieve its goals, not to give its directors financial gain

premier: the head of government in a province or territory in Canada

resign: to give up a position in a formal way

standardized tests: tests that ask all students the same questions and are graded the same way

transgender: a person who identifies as a different gender from the one assigned at birth

Selected Bibliography

"Asean Johnson, 9-Year-Old Chicago Student, SLAMS School Board for Massive Teacher Layoffs." *Huffington Post*, July 24, 2013. http://www.huffingtonpost.com/2013/07/24/asean-johnson-school-boar_n_3647474.html.

Erdely, Sabrina Rubin. "About a Girl: Coy Mathis' Fight to Change Gender." *Rolling Stone*, October 28, 2013. http://www.rollingstone.com/culture/news/about-a-girl-coy-mathis-fight-to-change-change-gender-20131028.

"Goodwill Ambassador-Hannah Godefa." UNICEF. Accessed August 25, 2015. http://www.unicef.org/ethiopia/about_12981.html.

"Malala Yousafzai." *Bio*. Accessed August 25, 2015. http://www.biography.com/people/malala-yousafzai-21362253.

Warner, Gregory, and Laura Starecheski. "Can't Afford School? Girls Learn to Negotiate the Harvard Way: #15Girls." *NPR*, October 8, 2015. http://www.npr.org/sections/goatsandsoda/2015/10/08/446237057/can-t-afford-school-girls-in-zambia-learn-to-negotiate-the-harvard-way-15girls.

Further Information

Class Size Matters
http://www.classsizematters.org
Learn why small classes can help kids learn better.

Doeden, Matt. *Malala Yousafzai: Shot by the Taliban, Still Fighting for Equal Education*. Minneapolis: Lerner Publications, 2015. Read more about Malala's brave fight to give all girls an education.

Dyslexie Font
http://www.dyslexiefont.com
Learn more about dyslexia and what makes Dyslexie a unique font.

The Malala Fund
http://www.malala.org
Learn more about Pakistani activist Malala Yousafzai.

Sandy Hook Promise
http://www.sandyhookpromise.org
Find out how Sandy Hook Promise is trying to keep kids safe from gun violence.

StopBullying.gov
http://www.stopbullying.gov/what-is-bullying
Learn more about the issue of bullying and find out how you can help stop bullying at your school.

Index

Photo Acknowledgments

The images in this book are used with the permission of: © panki/Shutterstock.com (sun burst background); © iStockphoto.com/billnoll (dot background); © Milos Djapovic/Shutterstock.com (grunge frame); © CataVic/Shutterstock.com, (crowd protest); © venimo/Shutterstock.com (megaphone); © photka/Shutterstock.com (protest sign) © kali9/E+/Getty Images, p. 4; © Kenneth Ilio/Flickr Vision/Getty Images, p. 5; © Anthony Souffle/Chicago Tribune/MC/Getty Images, p. 6; © Scott Olson/Getty Images, p. 7; © C. Bibby/Financial Times/REA/Redux, p. 8; © John Lamparski/Getty Images, p. 10; © iStockphoto.com/aimintang, p. 12; © 68/Ocean/ Corbis, p. 14; AP Photo/Las Cruces Sun-News/Robin Zielinski, p. 15; © Duel/ Cultura/Getty Images, p. 16; AP Photo/Henny Ray Abrams, p. 18; Courtesy Nancy McPhee/Stephen's Backpacks Society, pp. 20, 21; Anthony Behar/Sipa USA/Newscom, p. 22; © Oli Scarff/Getty Images, p. 23; © Dyslexie Font B.V., p. 24; © © Michael B. Thomas/Getty Images, p. 26; © Jill Torrannce/The New York Times/Redux, p. 29; © Christopher Furlong/Getty Images, p. 30; © Kevin Tachman/Wire Image/ Getty Images, p. 32; Courtesy of: Melanie Ross, pp. 36; Glen Stubbe/ZUMA Press/ Newscom, p. 37; AP Photo/Brandon Clark/ABImages, p. 38; AP Photo/PRNewsFoto/ Sandy Hook Promise, p. 39; © Tetra Images/Alamy, p. 42.

Front cover: © maglyvi/Shutterstock.com (school building); © panki/Shutterstock. com (sunburst background); © iStockphoto.com/billnoll (dot background); © Milos Djapovic/Shutterstock.com (grunge frame); © CataVic/Shutterstock.com (crowd protest); © venimo/Shutterstock.com (megaphone).

BOOK CHARGING CARD

Accession No. _____ Call No. _____

Author _____

Borrower's Name